A BOWL FULL of PEACE

A TRUE STORY

CAREN STELSON

ILLUSTRATED BY AKIRA KUSAKA

CAROLRHODA BOOKS
Minneapolis

TO YUI,
THIS STORY IS FOR YOU.
—C.S.

「つらい時代を乗り越えた、
全ての人々に敬意を持って。」

WITH RESPECT TO
ALL THOSE WHO
HAVE OVERCOME A
DIFFICULT TIME.
—A.K.

TO YUI,
THIS STORY IS FOR YOU.
—C.S.

いただきます

ITADAKIMASU

(EE-TAH-DAH-KEE-MAHS)

traditionally spoken before eating
a meal, this Japanese word means
"we humbly receive this food."

No one knows how old Grandmother's bowl is.
No one remembers who made it.
No one can count how many times
the bowl has passed from mother to daughter.

But everyone knows Grandmother's bowl is precious.

The city of Nagasaki sits along the Sea of Japan.
Mountains rise up around the harbor, and houses
made of wood with paper windows dot the hillsides.
On hot afternoons, Sachiko and her brothers Aki and Ichiro
chase dragonflies as cicadas buzz their summer song.

In the evenings, Sachiko's family gathers together.
Mother places Grandmother's bowl in the middle of the low table.
As always, the bowl offers good things to eat—
squid, eel, octopus, and udon noodles.
Sachiko and her family press their hands together
and bow their heads.
ITADAKIMASU, they whisper.

As Sachiko grows older, the sounds of war come to Nagasaki:
the clanging of hammers building torpedoes,
the marching of soldiers training for battle,
the cries of those whose husbands, fathers,
and brothers have been killed in the fighting.

War for Sachiko means less and less of everything.
Now Grandmother's bowl offers only
bits of mackerel floating in broth,
but the family is still together.
Even sister Misa and little Toshi learn to press their hands together.
ITADAKIMASU.

The sounds of war grow ever closer:
the grunts of boys and girls digging air-raid shelters into hillsides,
the wail of air-raid sirens echoing through the city,
the rumbles of enemy bombers flying overhead.
Sachiko is eager to start school, but after the first day, the school closes.
"Too dangerous," says the principal as he looks up at the sky.

The family still gathers each night for the evening meal.
Now Grandmother's bowl offers only wheat balls floating in boiled water.
Mother says, "Eat everything, children. Every bit is precious."
Sachiko and her family press their hands together and bow their heads.
ITADAKIMASU.

Summer comes again. The hot month of August arrives.
On August 9th, Sachiko's father visits a sick friend.
Mother prepares breakfast.
Aki, Ichiro, and Sachiko wait at the low table.
So do Misa and little Toshi.

Suddenly, the air-raid siren begins to wail.
Everyone runs for the shelter.
They leave everything behind—
even Grandmother's bowl.

Together, they huddle in the cave with their neighbors,
hoping no bomb will fall from the sky.

Finally, a siren blares all clear.
Everyone sighs.

Outside, Sachiko's friends ask if she would like to play house.
Yes, she would. Sachiko and her friends laugh together
and make mud dumplings with their small hands.

An enemy bomber rumbles high above the clouds.
No one notices until it is too late.

Sachiko looks around her.

What happened?

Father, Mother, Sachiko, and Misa survive.
Brothers Aki and Ichiro do too,
but not Toshi.
Little Toshi is killed in the blast.

Through the day and into the night, fires burn across the city.
Early in the morning, Sachiko's father makes a decision.
"We must leave Nagasaki. A train is coming to take us away
from the city. We must go *now*. Follow me."

Everywhere people are suffering.
"I'm so thirsty," voices whisper.

"Water, please, please water."

In a small hospital away from Nagasaki,
Sachiko's brothers are now very sick.
No one understands why.
No one understands it is because of the radiation from the bomb.
Aki dies. Then Ichiro dies.

Sachiko and sister Misa become ill.
So do Mother and Father.
Ice chips help soothe their burning throats,
but nothing can stop the pain,
not even the end of the war.

Two years pass before Sachiko's
family returns to Nagasaki.
Sachiko's father digs through the rubble
that was once their home.
Something glimmers in the dust.
Something green and shiny.
Grandmother's bowl!
It has survived without even a chip or crack.

Everyone in Sachiko's family has touched this bowl.
Everyone has eaten from it—
even Aki, Ichiro, and little Toshi.
At their evening meal, Sachiko's mother places
the precious bowl in the middle of a wooden crate.
Sachiko and her family press their hands together
and bow their heads.
ITADAKIMASU.

As cicadas sing their summer song,
another August 9th arrives.
In the morning, Sachiko's family kneels
in front of the wooden crate.
This time, Sachiko's mother fills
Grandmother's bowl with ice.

Sachiko's mother speaks softly,
"We must never forget what happened on this day.
Remember how a chip of ice eased our thirst?
As the ice melts, let us remember all who suffered
and all who died. We must pray that
such a terrible war never happens again."

Five years pass.
The radiation from the bomb makes
more people sick.
Sachiko's sister becomes ill and dies.

Another five years pass.
Sachiko's father becomes ill and dies.

Each August, Sachiko's mother fills Grandmother's bowl
with ice. Sachiko and her mother watch the ice melt.
Together, they remember what happened.
Together, they pray for peace.

Then Sachiko's mother becomes ill and dies.

In August, Sachiko fills Grandmother's bowl with ice.
She bows her head as the ice melts.

Grandmother's bowl is now Sachiko's to care for.

Sachiko fills Grandmother's bowl with
good things to eat just as her mother did.
She presses her hands together and bows her head.
ITADAKIMASU.

One August 9th, fifty years after the war's end,
Sachiko fills Grandmother's bowl with ice.
She can no longer be silent about what happened to her.
She must tell her story.
The world must know that such a bomb
can never be used again.

That evening, Sachiko stands before a group of children
and shares her story for the first time. She begins,
"What happened to me must never happen to you."

And the children listen.

AUTHOR'S NOTE

The story in this book has been close to my heart for many years. Between 2010 and 2015, I made five visits to Nagasaki and spent many hours interviewing Sachiko Yasui about her experience as a survivor of the atomic bomb during World War II to write the book, *Sachiko: A Nagasaki Bomb Survivor's Story*. The more Sachiko told me about her grandmother's bowl, the more I knew the bowl had its own story to tell.

Sachiko was only six years old on August 9, 1945, when the atomic bomb detonated over her city of Nagasaki. She was playing outside with her friends a mere 900 meters, about a half mile, from ground zero. Few people survived the bombing that close to the explosion—her playmates were all killed. Buildings were destroyed, including Sachiko's own home. Sachiko's family had to leave Nagasaki for a time. When they returned to their home to rebuild, everyone was greatly surprised as Sachiko's father pulled Grandmother's bowl from the rubble. The bowl had survived without a chip or crack. As Sachiko told me, the bowl had the fingerprints of all the members of her family on it. Despite war, death, and suffering, Grandmother's bowl brought Sachiko's family together again.

Clockwise from top left: Sachiko Yasui, age five. Sachiko's grandmother holds baby Ichiro, and young Aki stands near an aunt. Sachiko shares her story with students in Japan, many of whom hold strings of origami cranes, which represent peace.

To help tell this story, I included the Japanese word *itadakimasu* (いただきます). Rooted in Japanese Buddhism, *itadakimasu* means, "I humbly receive." Each time I visited Sachiko in Nagasaki, we shared meals together, often a delicious array of fresh fish, eel, octopus, and udon noodles. Before beginning to eat, we pressed our hands together and whispered, "*Itadakimasu*." (I humbly receive this food.) As I read more about *itadakimasu*, I grew to appreciate the word's greater meaning: I am grateful for everything and everyone who made this meal possible. At the heart of *itadakimasu* is gratitude. I am grateful for my friendship with Sachiko. She taught me about the strength to live as a *hibakusha*, an atomic bomb survivor; the determination needed to find a path to peace; and the courage it takes to tell one's story as an eyewitness to nuclear war.

No one can fully appreciate a story such as Sachiko's without knowing something about the history of World War II (1939–1945) and the grim events of the Pacific War. The Pacific War was deadly for all sides—both the Allied powers (which included the United States) and the Axis powers (which included Japan). As World War II neared its end, the United States dropped atomic bombs over two Japanese cities. On August 6, 1945, the crew of the US B-29 bomber *Enola Gay* flew above the city of Hiroshima, detonating an atomic bomb with the equivalent force of 15,000 tons of TNT. With one bomb, 140,000 people were killed and 90 percent of the city was destroyed. Three days later, the crew of the B-29 bomber *Bockscar* flew above the city of Nagasaki. This second atomic bomb, with an equivalent force of 21,000 tons of TNT, killed approximately 74,000 people. During each detonation, many people, including Sachiko's youngest brother, Toshi, were wounded or killed by glass, wood, and metal flying through the air, propelled by the bomb's blast. Many others died from flash burns and severe radiation exposure from the nuclear explosion. Soon after the atomic bombings, World War II came to an end, but the end of the war did not end the suffering of the atomic bomb survivors. In the months and years that followed, many more survivors would die from radiation sickness and cancers from radiation exposure.

GRANDMOTHER'S BOWL IN 2019

The United States' decision to use the atomic bomb as a weapon of war changed the world forever. We know that nuclear weapons must never be used again, yet thousands of nuclear weapons exist in the world's arsenals today. These present-day nuclear weapons are far more powerful than the ones detonated over Hiroshima and Nagasaki. In 2017, the International Campaign to Abolish Nuclear Weapons (ICAN) received the Nobel Peace Prize for its role in achieving the United Nations Treaty on the Prohibition of Nuclear Weapons to outlaw nuclear weapons around the world. Until nuclear weapons are eliminated, every August 9 I will fill my own "Grandmother's bowl" with ice and imagine all those who know Sachiko's story filling their "Grandmother's bowls" too. As the ice melts, may we pray for peace, believe in peace, and work toward world peace, for the benefit of everyone.

—CAREN STELSON

ILLUSTRATOR'S NOTE *(included in English and the illustrator's original Japanese)*

I belong to a generation that has not experienced war. Our knowledge of war comes primarily from history classes in school. Textbooks covered the First and Second World Wars, the misery that Japan caused, and the misery that Japan endured.

As a result, many people of my generation think of war as "an incident from a textbook" and feel that it is something that happens only in a movie or a novel. I am one of them. I think I understand the horror of war and the threat of nuclear weapons, but I do not believe I can truly understand how terrible a real-life war is.

When I received the offer to illustrate this book, I was nervous. I wondered if I, who have not experienced war, should accept. However, I also wondered how many opportunities in life I would have to illustrate such a story. I realized it might be a chance for me to learn about war afresh. It was a challenge.

As I illustrated Sachiko's story, I was reminded of my grandmother, who experienced war in her youth. She told me about the lack of food, about being burned out of her home, about the battle to survive.

My grandmother passed away many years ago. Japan too will soon lose all the people who have experienced war. There will be no more living witnesses left. That is why Sachiko's story of surviving the atomic bomb is especially important.

War is still present in our world. We still have to fear nuclear weapons. Even the threat of war causes damage and division between people and nations.

I truly hope this story will inspire you to think about peace and that Sachiko's hope for peace will be passed along to you and to future generations to come.

—AKIRA KUSAKA 日下 明

私は戦争を知らない世代です。この世代の人々の多くは、学校の歴史の授業で戦争について学びます。第一次・第二次世界大戦はもちろんの事、日本が起こした悲惨な事、日本で起きた悲惨な事。その時代の世界情勢など、現代の子供達の教科書にもその事実が書かれています。

そのため、今の平和になった日本、特に戦争を知らない世代にとって、戦争とは「教科書に載っている事」という認識が強く、どこか映画や小説を読んでいる感覚に近いのではと思います。かく言う私もそんな世代の一人で、頭の中では戦争なんて絶対ダメだとか、核の脅威も分かったつもりでいますが、戦争の真の恐ろしさを理解していないと思います。

この本の依頼をいただいた時、戦争を知らない私が、人々に伝わる絵が描けるのか不安もありました。ですがこの先、私のイラストレーターとしての人生の中で、このテーマで絵を描く事が何度あるだろうか…。戦争を知らないからこそ、私自身が改めて学ぶ機会になるのではないかと思い、挑戦させていただきました。

幸子さんの物語を絵にする過程で、私は祖母の話を思い出しました。祖母は若い頃に戦争を体験しています。私は幼い頃、祖母から戦中・戦後の話をよく聞かされました。それは食糧難や家を焼け出された事、戦争がきっかけで引き起こる、人と人との醜い争いの話でした。

そんな祖母も、もう何年も前に亡くなり、もうすぐ日本には戦争を体験した世代がいなくなります。戦争を経験した生き証人がいなくなる時代だからこそ、私たちには幸子さんの被爆体験を記したこの本が必要です。

今現在もまだどこかで戦争は起きていて、その脅威は無くなっていません。この物語の中心である「核」の脅威もまだまだ残っています。戦争がもたらす脅威は実質的な被害だけでなく、人と人との繋がりも引き裂きます。

この物語が、平和について考えるきっかけになる事を、そして幸子さんの平和への思いが私たち、またはその後に続く世代にも伝わる事を願っています。

RECOMMENDED BOOKS

Halperin, Wendy Anderson. *Peace*. New York: Atheneum Books for Young Readers, 2013.
Weaving a famous poem by Chinese philosopher Lao-tzu ("For there to be peace in the world . . .") with quotations from a wide range of peacemakers and intricate illustrated pages of everyday life, this picture book invites young readers to ponder the many pathways to world peace.

Kaneko, Misuzu. Illustrated by Toshikado Hajiri. *Are You an Echo? The Lost Poetry of Misuzu Kaneko*. Seattle: Chin Music, 2016.
When poet Misuzu Kaneko's journals were destroyed in the firebombing of Tokyo during World War II, her sensitive and inquisitive poetry seemed to be lost forever. *Are You an Echo?* reveals the story of Misuzu's difficult life and the rediscovery of beloved poems she wrote as a young woman. Misuzu's illustrated poetry brings to life scenes of nature and yearning young readers will appreciate and enjoy.

Loske, Judith. *Sadako's Cranes*. Hong Kong: Minedition (Michael Neugebauer), 2015.
With elegant illustrations and simple text, Loske retells the story of young Sadako Sasaki, who lived in Hiroshima and developed leukemia ten years after the atomic bombing of her city. Inspired by an ancient Japanese legend, Sadako embarks on a goal to fold one thousand origami paper cranes to make her wish for health come true. After Sadako's death, a monument honoring her was built in Hiroshima Peace Memorial Park.

Popov, Nikolai. *Why?* Hong Kong: Minedition (Michael Neugebauer), 1996.
Popov has created a wordless and profound picture book that explores war and peace at a level young children can grasp.

Reibstein, Mark. Illustrated by Ed Young. *Wabi Sabi*. New York: Little, Brown, 2008.
Wabi Sabi, a curious Japanese cat, takes off on a journey to find the deeper meaning of her name. This beautifully textured book invites young readers into the richness of Japanese culture.

Tsuchiya, Yukio. Illustrated by Ted Lewin. *Faithful Elephants: A True Story of Animals, People, and War*. Boston: Houghton Mifflin, 1988.
The tragic account of the elephants in the Tokyo Zoo during World War II is a classic story about the trauma of war for both animals and people—and the need for world peace.

Acknowledgments

It's impossible to list in this space the many people, both in Japan and the United States, who helped me understand and write Sachiko Yasui's story. Let me begin with the people to whom I am most indebted: First, I must thank Sachiko Yasui for the trust she placed in me to tell her story; Etsuko Matsuo, for her steadfast support; Dr. Takayuki Miyanishi and Fumiko Yamaguchi, President and Vice President, respectively, of the Nagasaki-Saint Paul Sister Cities Committee for their valuable time, translations, and friendship throughout all my work with Sachiko; JoAnn Blatchley, President of the St. Paul-Nagasaki Sister City Committee; Keiko Kawakami, Teaching Specialist of Japanese at the University of Minnesota, for her translations and keen insights into Japanese culture; Carol Hinz, Editorial Director, and Danielle Carnito, Art Director, at Carolrhoda/Lerner Publishing Group, for their exceptional bookmaking visions and continued belief in the importance of Sachiko's story. My heartfelt gratitude to my husband, Kim, who knew all along how important Sachiko's story was to tell. —C.S.

Text copyright © 2020 by Caren Stelson
Illustrations copyright © 2020 by Akira Kusaka

Carolrhoda Books®
An imprint of Lerner Publishing Group, Inc.
241 First Avenue North
Minneapolis, MN 55401 USA

For reading levels and more information, look up this title at www.lernerbooks.com.

Photo credits: Family photos courtesy of Sachiko Yasui, p. 36 (all); Bowl photo Todd Strand/Independent Picture Service, p. 37.

Designed by Danielle Carnito.
Main body text set in Futura Std Book. Typeface provided by Adobe Systems.
The illustrations in this book were painted digitally.

Library of Congress Cataloging-in-Publication Data

Names: Stelson, Caren Barzelay, author. | Kusaka, Akira, 1981– illustrator.
Title: A bowl full of peace : a true story / Caren Stelson ; illustrated by Akira Kusaka.
Description: Minneapolis : Carolrhoda Books, [2020] | Audience: Ages: 7–11. | Audience: Grades: K–3. | Includes bibliographical references.
Identifiers: LCCN 2019011878 (print) | LCCN 2019018081 (ebook) | ISBN 9781541582194 (eb pdf) | ISBN 9781541521483 (lb : alk. paper)
Subjects: LCSH: Yasui, Sachiko—Juvenile literature. | Atomic bomb victims—Japan—Nagasaki-shi—Biography—Juvenile literature. | Nagasaki-shi (Japan)—History—Bombardment, 1945—Juvenile literature. | World War, 1939–1945—Japan—Nagasaki-shi—Juvenile literature.
Classification: LCC D767.25.N3 (ebook) | LCC D767.25.N3 S73 2020 (print) | DDC 940.54/252244092 [B]—dc23

LC record available at https://lccn.loc.gov/2019011878

Manufactured in the United States of America
1-44377-34642-8/5/2019